Ready, Set, Daven!

A Guided Journal:
Daily Thoughts to Inspire
Your Davening

C. Liba Rimler

ACKNOWLEDGMENTS, PERMISSIONS & COPYRIGHT

Thank you to Rabbi Benyomin Simpson for his assistance in reviewing the material and making suggestions for this project.
Thank you to Chani Fishman and Bailey Goldstein for their guidance in editing and proofreading.

All information in this book has been carefully compiled from Torah sources and adapted from outside sources with permission from the publishers. Please refer to bibliography on page 183 to see credits and list of resources for further reading.

All journal writing prompts are original.

Great effort has been made to preserve accuracy of content; however, minor contextual details in stories may have been changed, intentionally or unintentionally.

The images in this book are from Pixabay (commercial use permitted and no attribution required).

To leave a rating or review, visit the Ready, Set, Daven! product page on Amazon.

ISBN: 9798666104576

Cover by Michal Rimler

A NOTE TO THE READER

This journal is dedicated with gratitude towards my students at Cheder Chabad of Monsey—past, present, and future—for whom I create and implement these lessons. With great thanks to Hashem, it is a privilege to have been able to produce this for the use of educators and students outside the four walls of my own classroom.

The learning contained in this project is לעילוי נשמת צבי בן שאול, my maternal grandfather (Zvi Shkedi), who passed away shortly before this book was completed.
One of the things he was known for was his reverence for תפילה. I still have a vision in my mind of him wrapped in Tefillin by his special table, reciting the Shema with complete concentration. When my grandfather davened, the time was sacred. It was as if nothing else existed at the moment.

It is my hope that this journal will help others experience the same feelings of sanctity during davening that he did.

May we merit to greet Moshiach speedily in our days.

C. Liba Rimler
Teves 5781
Pomona, New York

It is said: "המתפלל בעד חבירו הוא נענה תחילה"
"One who prays for his friend is answered first".

אברהם אבינו davened that Hashem should heal
אבימלך and his family.

Because of this, "וה' פקד את שרה" — "Hashem
remembered שרה". In turn, she and אברהם were
blessed with a son.

Hashem answers the תפילות of those who daven
for others.
Today, devote your davening to someone else.

Who would you like to daven for today?

_____

What would you like Hashem to grant them?

_____

_____

_____

_____

Once, a farmer was blessed that he would be granted a successful crop.

However, he neither plowed nor planted his fields. So of course, no matter how much rain and sunshine his field received, nothing grew.

היום יום כ"ה חשון

וועֶן מעֶן אַקעֶרט און מעֶן פאַרזיֵיט — וואַקסט

"When you plow and you sow, things will grow".

Hashem has plenty of blessings in store for us. It is our job to daven in order to bring those blessings down. Davening requires effort. It's therefore important to visualize all the goodness that Hashem has in store!

What do you hope Hashem will grant you today?

_____

A young prince lived in a small cottage near the king's castle. One day, robbers came and destroyed his home.

Crying bitterly, the prince begged for his father to rebuild his cottage. The king took no action, despite his son's pleas.

Disappointed, the prince asked his father why he refused to help him.

The king answered, "On the contrary, I want to help you! I will indeed do so. The reason I have not rebuilt your cottage is because I want to build you a palace in its place."

Hashem sometimes chooses not to immediately answer a request because He has something better in store.

Give an example.

_____

_____

Once, a famous doctor spoke at a medical conference about an issue she encountered among her patients. Many people would faint upon awakening.

How did she help them? She told them to sit up in bed for 12 seconds before standing up.

A Jewish person in the audience exclaimed, excited, "We do that every day!"

מודה אני has 12 words. It takes 12 seconds when you say it with כוונה.

Taking these moments to be grateful to Hashem for giving you life each morning really makes a difference in your day.

What are you thankful to Hashem for giving you today? List 4 things.

1. _____

2. _____

3. _____

4. _____

וַאֲנִי בְּרֹב חַסְדְּךָ אָבוֹא בֵיתֶךָ
אֶשְׁתַּחֲוֶה אֶל הֵיכַל קָדְשְׁךָ בְּיִרְאָתֶךָ

And I, with Your great kindness, will come to Your house; I will bow towards Your holy sanctuary in awe of You

Before beginning to daven, envision yourself entering the בית המקדש.

You are about to speak directly to Hashem Himself.

Write a diary entry describing the feelings of someone who is about to enter the בית המקדש. What sights do they see? What thoughts are running through their mind?

_____

_____

_____

_____

_____

One day, a composer is hit with a sudden flash of inspiration. He hears a beautiful melody in his head. He sits down at the piano and works out the precise notes and phrasing that will bring his song to life. It's going to be a stunning masterpiece of music. He can't wait to debut it at his next concert.

What would happen if the musician wouldn't play his song out loud? You can only imagine the disappointment the audience would feel if they showed up to his concert, to see him just sitting there, staring at the notes.

And so it is with davening.

The words on the pages of the סידור must be verbalized.
It is important to read each word carefully in order to properly connect with Hashem.

Which תפילה will you focus on reading aloud today?

הריני מקבל עלי מצוות עשה של ואהבת לרעך כמוך

"I accept upon myself the commandment to love my fellow Jew as I love myself."

Q: Why do we say this *before* we begin davening?

A: When a father sees his children getting along with each other, it fills him with the desire to give. **When Hashem sees that we, His children, are united, it fills Him with the desire to answer our תפילות.**

Write down the name of one person you take upon yourself to reach out to today.

_____

How will you reach out?

_____

When the Frierdiker Rebbe was a young boy, he asked his grandmother Rebbetzin Rivka why it takes his father such a long time to daven. She answered:

"Your father is a great חסיד and צדיק, and he thinks about the meaning of each word of davening before saying it."

Open your סידור to a תפילה which you have a habit of saying very quickly. Today, take a few minutes to say the words slowly, concentrating on the meaning. What will you think about when saying it?

_____

_____

_____

_____

Riding a bicycle uphill takes effort. But as long as there is forward movement — even if there are bumps along the way — you are moving, making progress.

However, if the bicycle stops, it will not stand still; it will slide back down the mountain.

It is the same with davening. It is a constant עבודה. You need to work hard to stay on track. **You don't have to be perfect, but as long as you are constantly going in the right direction, you will succeed.**

Draw a picture illustrating the example, and write a caption about what you can do to inspire your davening today.

As Rabbi Akiva was being tortured by the Romans, he calmly began to recite שמע with complete joy. His students were shocked by Rabbi Akiva's serenity and exclaimed, "Our teacher, how can you remain so calm and concentrate on שמע when you are being tortured?"

Rabbi Akiva answered, "My entire life I was bothered by the fact that I never had the opportunity to fulfill the verse:
"ואהבת את ה' ...ובכל נפשך" *'You shall love Hashem ... with all your soul'.*
Now, I finally have the chance to fulfill it!"

~~

When you love someone, you are willing to give things up to make them happy. (For example: a mother gives up her sleep to take care of her child.) **Davening is a time to think about how you can devote your life to Hashem.** When an opportunity to do so arises, you will be fully prepared.

What can YOU "give" to serve Hashem?

_____

_____

Reb Elimelech of Lizhensk would say the following words before entering the Shul to daven:

"Know where you are entering;
what you will do there;
Who is in this house;
Whose house it is;
and Who empowered you to enter this house."

Why do you think Reb Elimelech said these words before he went to Shul?

_____

_____

Your mother asks to you bring her a cup of tea. You go out of your way to prepare it for her, choosing the flavor that she likes and adding just the right amount of sweetener. As you bring the steaming mug over to her and see her smile, you feel pleased to have fulfilled your mother's desire. It feels good to bring her pleasure.

~~~

Before performing any מצוה — even if we don't understand all the specifics — **we should have the כוונה in mind that we are fulfilling this מצוה because Hashem instructed us to do so; and that we are doing it in order to bring pleasure to Him.** In turn, Hashem's love towards us will be aroused.

How will you daven in a way that brings pleasure to Hashem today?

_____

_____

A king once asked his son to transfer a very heavy stone to the tower of the palace. No matter how the prince tried, he couldn't figure out a way to lift such a huge boulder, let alone get it up the tower.

Finally, the king said, "Do you really think I expect you to carry it in one piece? Chip away at the stone with a chisel and hammer. Each day bring up some pieces. This is how you will bring up the entire stone: one piece at a time!"

Davening is a process. It is not a "quick fix". משה רבינו kept davening for forty days until Hashem finally forgave the Jews for the חטא עגל הזהב, the sin of the golden calf.

~~~

Why do you think משה רבינו had to daven for so long before Hashem granted forgiveness?

_____

_____

The Frierdiker Rebbe once related:

"Once, after returning from a walk with my father, he reminded me of a busy street corner we had passed.

"At that spot," he said to me, "I suddenly had an intense and inspiring thought. I believe this is because long ago, a Jew once davened מנחה at this spot."

That Jew may have davened with less than ideal concentration, being that it was a busy street. Yet his holy תפילות purified the air so that when my father walked through that area many years later, his mind was able to sense it."

You elevate the ground and the entire area around you when you daven.

List some places you've davened at.

Digging for Gold: A משל

Once, a person heard a rumor that there might be gold buried in his backyard. Excited to see if it was true, he began to dig. After many hours, he began to doubt that the gold was even there. So he decided that the rumor was false, and put away his shovel.

The second person knew for certain that there was gold buried somewhere in his backyard, so he never gave up. He dug up every inch of soil, and when that did not yield the treasure, he dug deeper and deeper. He felt that his effort was worthwhile, because he knew he would eventually succeed and find great wealth. Indeed, he did find the treasure in the end.

What would you say to encourage someone who feels like davening is hard work?

_____

_____

_____

The word "תפל" means "connect". **When we daven, we form a bond between ourselves and our Creator.**

Another word has the same root as the word "תפילה". It is "תפילין"!

The מצוות of תפילין and davening both serve as powerful ways for us to strengthen our bond with Hashem.

Hashem is our Father. It brings Him joy to hear from us every day!

What can you tell yourself to feel connected to Hashem when you daven today?

Rabbi Schneur Zalman of Liadi, the Alter Rebbe, was once traveling and reached a fork in the road.

The Alter Rebbe recounted: "I had to decide where to go. I knew that in Vilna one was taught how to learn, and that in Mezeritch one could learn how to daven. To learn I was somewhat able, but of davening I knew very little. So I went to Mezeritch. Hashem blessed me with making the right choice. I became a devoted student of our Rebbe's, and when I returned to Vitebsk, I guided my students in the teachings of חסידות, which were well received by them."

Why did the Alter Rebbe decide to go to Mezeritch?

_____

_____

In the year 1951, a man came to daven at the Shul in 770 together with his six-year-old son. As מנחה was about to begin, the young boy started looking for a סידור. Davening had already begun, but the boy was still empty-handed.

Making his way back toward his father, he saw another man inviting him to come share his סידור. This man was none other than the Lubavitcher Rebbe. The boy sat down next to the Rebbe, and together they began to daven from the same סידור.

The חסידים were uncomfortable with this. They motioned to the child to to return to his father. When the Rebbe realized what was happening, he looked at the חסידים and said, **"What do you want from him? My תפילות are going up to שמים very nicely when he davens with me!"**

What would you title this story?

"   "

שמונה עשרה, has 18 blessings. Some say this corresponds to the 18 vertebrae of the spine.

When one davens, the entire body has to be involved. When one bows during שמונה עשרה, one should bend over so that the bones of the spine protrude.

List the ways you can involve other parts of your body in your davening.

Eyes	
Ears	
Mouth	
Hands	
Feet	

When a mother comes to wake her child for school in the morning, she knows she is about to bring him out of his peaceful slumber. She wishes she could let him lie there until his eyes open on their own. However, she knows how much her child has to accomplish that day. She knocks on the door, but he doesn't hear. So she lovingly calls his name, and he still doesn't flinch. Finally, she taps him on the shoulder. Startled, he wakes up.

"Thanks!" he says. She leaves the room. Her mission is complete.

Sometimes, Hashem has to "wake" us up by making our lives a little uncomfortable. We need to recognize that this is coming from Hashem's love. Hashem does this so that we will turn to Him with our תפילות.

Write an example of a challenge that would remind a person to daven with more passion.

_____

_____

_____

A Jewish man traveling on the road once stopped to daven שמונה עשרה. A Roman officer came riding by and greeted him, but he did not reply. Infuriated, the officer waited for him to finish davening, and then yelled at him, "Why didn't you talk to me? I could have killed you!" The Jew replied with a question, **"If you would be standing in front of a king, and your friend would pass by to greet you, would you even turn your head to speak?"**

"Of course not!"

"And if you would reply, what would be done to you?" "I would be killed!" said the minister. "I was standing in prayer before the King of all kings," the Jew explained. "How could I stop to greet you?"

The Roman thought for a moment. "You're right!" he said. He now understood why the man had not greeted him.

No longer angry, he allowed the Jew to continue his journey in peace.

Why didn't the Jew return the Roman's greeting?

Have you ever thought about the motion of a bow and arrow?

The closer you pull the bow towards your heart, the further the arrow catapults.

So too is with davening. **The more you focus inwards, the further your תפילות will soar.**

Davening is a time to focus on your נשמה. Take advantage of this time to think deeply about your connection with Hashem.
You will feel a difference in your day. You will have more energy and you will be motivated to serve Him.

What does your נשמה want to accomplish?

_____

_____

From the רמב"ם:

משנה תורה

מִצְוַת עֲשֵׂה לְהִתְפַּלֵּל בְּכָל יוֹם

It is a positive commandment to daven every

_____,

שֶׁנֶּאֱמַר (שמות כג כה) "וַעֲבַדְתֶּם אֵת ה' אֱלֹקֵיכֶם"

As it _____, "And you should serve Hashem, your G-d."

מִפִּי הַשְּׁמוּעָה לָמְדוּ שֶׁעֲבוֹדָה זוֹ הִיא תְּפִלָּה.

According to what we learn, this service is prayer.

שֶׁנֶּאֱמַר (דברים יא יג) "וּלְעָבְדוֹ בְּכָל לְבַבְכֶם"

As it says, "And you should serve Him with all your _____."

אָמְרוּ חֲכָמִים אֵי זוֹ הִיא עֲבוֹדָה שֶׁבַּלֵּב זוֹ תְּפִלָּה

Our sages say, what is this "_____ of the heart"? It is prayer.

Work out the גימטריה below:

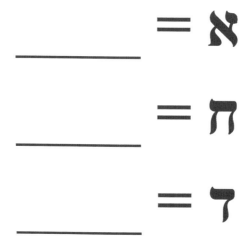

$$\text{א} = \underline{\hspace{4cm}}$$

$$\text{ח} = \underline{\hspace{4cm}}$$

$$\text{ד} = \underline{\hspace{4cm}}$$

When saying "אחד 'ה" in שמע, one should think about the fact that Hashem is the only Ruler over the seven heavens, the earth, and the four directions of the globe.

ה' = Hashem was, is, and will be: היה, הווה, ויהיה

א = Hashem is One,

ח = over the seven heavens and one earth,

ד = and the four directions of the globe.

You receive greater reward for going to shul in stormy weather than when the sun is shining, because it shows your devotion.

In such a time, you are not going to shul just for a nice walk; you are going out of commitment to Hashem.

Why do you think it is important to daven and show your commitment to Hashem specifically when it's not easy?

_____

_____

_____

_____

_____

_____

_____

In בראשית, we are told that Hashem planned to inform אברהם אבינו about what would happen to סדום.

Hashem knew that אברהם would daven for the city. And indeed, אברהם continued to daven on behalf of סדום, even after the מלאכים left to destroy the city.

It took many generations for his תפילות to produce positive results. Only לוט and his two daughters survived the destruction of סדום. Many generations later, רות, a descendant, became the great-grandmother of דוד המלך.

The תפילות of אברהם were finally answered. No תפילה ever goes to waste!

Why do you think Hashem sometimes saves our תפילות for another time?

_____

_____

_____

_____

A mother asks her child to go from the basement to get an object from the attic. She won't be upset when the child doesn't get there in a split second.
She understands that her child can only go upstairs one step at a time.

Hashem is patient with us. So too, we should be patient with ourselves. Celebrate every accomplishment in your davening. The main thing is to keep on growing.

Create a step-by-step plan with small davening goals for the next four days.

1. _____

2. _____

3. _____

4. _____

We can speak to Hashem in our own language in the section by **שמע קולינו**, before the words **כי אתה שומע**. **It is a place to make personal requests.**

Write a letter to Hashem.
Include some personal requests.

_____

_____

_____

_____

_____

_____

_____

_____

אלקנה had two wives, חנה and פנינה.

While פנינה had children, חנה had none. The family lived in ארץ ישראל, and would visit the משכן in שילה once a year.

On one of the visits, חנה stood and davened that Hashem bless her with a son. **Quietly whispering, pouring out her heart, she made a promise that if she was blessed with a son, she would dedicate his entire life to Hashem.**

עלי הכהן walked in and thought she was drunk. He saw her moving her lips, and no sound was coming out! He rebuked her for entering the משכן in such a condition.

But חנה answered him calmly, telling him that she was not drunk. Rather, she was pouring her heart out to Hashem.

Why do you think חנה was whispering?

_____

_____

עלי הכהן blessed חנה that Hashem should hear her תפילות.

Indeed, her heartfelt requests were answered. Within a short time, she gave birth to a son, who became שמואל הנביא, who lived a life dedicated to Hashem.

Like חנה, we daven quietly by שמונה עשרה. This is our private time between ourselves and Hashem.

חנה davened with emotion. She didn't worry about what others would think, even though it was unusual at the time to daven quietly. And in the end, Hashem answered her.

Jot down a few private thoughts you want to share with Hashem today.

_____

_____

_____

_____

Story: The Father and Son (Part 1)

Once, a father and his young son were traveling to a distant city. On the way, they came to a stream. Turning to his father, the son complained, "Abba, it's too deep for me. I can't cross this stream." The father answered, "Don't worry, son. I will take care of you." Immediately, he lifted his son, carrying him across the stream. They continued onwards. Suddenly, they were attacked by a band of robbers. The father said, "Son, stand behind me, and you will be safe." The child obeyed, and with the stick he was holding, the father fought the robbers off. The father and his son continued on their way, but soon came to a high fence.

"Abba, how will I climb over this fence?" the boy asked. His father replied, "Don't worry, son," and, taking the boy on his shoulders, he climbed the fence with him.

Can you think of a time Hashem 'carried' you?

_____

_____

Story: The Father and Son (Part 2)

When finally they reached their destination, they found the city gates locked. They searched everywhere for a way to enter. Suddenly, the father cried, "Son, look! There is a small opening. I'm not able to get through it, but you can."

Gently, he continued, "My child, I've carried you and taken care of you on this entire journey. Now it is your turn to help me. This opening is too small for me, but you'll be able to fit through it. Once you are inside, you can open the door for me!"

In the same way, said the Dubner Maggid, at times the gates of תפילה are closed to adults. Children are pure. They are able to enter the small opening that remains.

"Go in, dear children," he would say, "and open the gates for us. Daven for us. Your תפילות will be accepted."

Why do you think Hashem loves to hear from children?

FIRE REQUIRES FUEL. Even the

brightest, most impressive bonfire needs to be
constantly fed to keep it alive.

So too, you must constantly "fuel" your desire
to serve Hashem by doing positive actions.

Don't wait for the feelings to come. Act first.

**The act of davening itself leads you to feel
more inspired and connected to Hashem.**

Draw a picture of a bonfire.
*Write a caption about what feelings you hope
will come when you daven today.*

The גוף (body) holds the נשמה (soul), and the נשמה gives life to the גוף.

The words you say from the סידור are like the גוף. **Understanding the meaning of the words is like the נשמה.**

It is important to say the words even if you don't understand them all right away, as the words of the סידור are holy.

Still, make sure to learn a little bit each day so that your תפילות are richer. In regard to what you don't understand, ask Hashem to have the כוונות in mind for you; for when you daven with your mouth but you are busy thinking about other things unrelated to davening, your תפילה is like a גוף without a נשמה.

Why is it important to have the meaning in mind?

_____

_____

_____

Your boss gives you money for a specific project, and warns you against using it for any other purpose.

He explains that he will demand records of your expenses at the end of the year, so he will know what you used the money for.

Hashem gives us life: a נשמה and a body to use in this world, as well as many other things we need in order to serve Him.

Davening is a great time to think about where we are holding — and whether we are serving Hashem as we should.

Where in davening will you concentrate on this idea today? Describe why you have chosen this תפילה (how it connects).

_____

_____

_____

_____

Imagine that as an infant, you are abandoned in the street. A passing stranger sees you and takes pity on you. He brings you home and takes care of you until you are a grown adult.

Imagine how obligated you would feel towards this person and how much you would owe them in every way.

Hashem cares for you and provides for all your needs. Thinking about this will motivate you to serve Him and do his מצוות.

Write a thank-you letter to Hashem!

מלחמה פנימית :The Inner Battle

כִּי תֵצֵא לַמִּלְחָמָה עַל אֹיְבֶיךָ

"When you go out to war against your enemies"

This phrase refers to the war between man and his יצר הרע.

The זוהר states:

"שעת צלותא שעת קרבא"

"The time of davening is a time of war"

Why is davening a "war"? Isn't it a time to ask for our personal needs? Who are we fighting against?

What do you think the "war" is, and how do we fight this battle?

_____

_____

_____

מלחמה פנימית: The Inner Battle

Q: It would make sense for people to only daven when they need something. What is the purpose of having set times for תפילה every single day?

A: Our חכמים compare תפילה to קרבנות.

We daven <u>every day</u> as a substitute for the קרבן תמיד, which was brought <u>every day</u>.

Does your davening experience feel the same or different every day? Why or why not?

_____

_____

_____

_____

_____

_____

מלחמה פנימית: The Inner Battle

Every Jewish person has two souls:

1) The נפש אלוקית, which is an actual part of Hashem. The נפש אלוקית wants to serve Hashem.

2) The נפש הבהמית, which is the animal soul. The נפש הבהמית wants us to take care of our bodies.

Bringing a קרבן meant that a person had to bring an animal sacrifice on the מזבח.

Nowadays, we cannot bring קרבנות since we do not have a בית המקדש. So instead, we daven, bringing up the "animal" soul, the נפש הבהמית, to Hashem.

Describe what it would feel like to go to the בית המקדש and bring a קרבן.

_____

_____

מלחמה פנימית: **The Inner Battle**

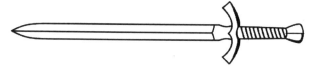

When a Yid would bring a קרבן, a fire would come down from above (as a sign that Hashem accepted their offering).

The goal of תפילה is like a קרבן — to bring up the <u>animal</u> soul, the נפש הבהמית, for Hashem.

Our נפש הבהמית is focused on our bodies' survival and desires. It gets us to do things like eat, sleep, and play. It gets us excited about physical things. **When we get the נפש הבהמית to take pleasure in connecting with Hashem, this is the greatest gift we can bring!**

How does your נפש הבהמית help you daven?

_____

_____

_____

מלחמה פנימית‎: The Inner Battle

The אש דקדושה‎, the fire of holiness, is the fire of אהבת ה'‎ that is awakened in a person at the time of davening. This "holy fire" turns a person away from following the "fire" of the temptations of this world.

We need to convert the fire of the יצר הרע‎ to a fire of holiness. We need to use the passion of our physical selves — our energy, love, and excitement — to serve Hashem.

So, this is the מלחמה‎ within davening. The war is to fight the fire of the יצר הרע‎ with the fire of קדושה‎. This is accomplished through תפילה‎.

Write about a time you felt really excited to do a מצוה‎. What physical senses did you use?

_____

_____

_____

_____

מלחמה פנימית: The Inner Battle

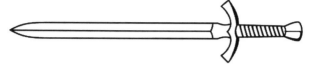

The אריז"ל taught that every object in this world has a spark of קדושה inside it.
But Hashem chose not to reveal these sparks.
He wants us to find the treasure ourselves.
Every נשמה has specific sparks that it needs to elevate scattered around the world. Our job is to take the sparks out of גלות. The sparks of קדושה are trapped, waiting to be freed, and it is up to us to finish the task.

Now let us return to our original question.
Q: Why do we have to daven *every single day?*
A: Every day a new spark needs to be elevated.
We wake up to a fresh challenge every morning, as it says:
"יצרו של אדם מתגבר עליו בכל יום"
"A person's יצר הרע strengthens against him daily." This is the war we fight during davening: the battle of redirecting the fire of the נפש הבהמית to serve Hashem.

Why do we have to daven every day?

_____

Hashem hid sparks of קדושה all over the world.

Whenever a person davens with כוונה, his words attract one of these lost sparks and sends it heavenward to add brilliance and sparkle to Hashem's magnificent crown.

Each word of תפילה is a precious gem with which Hashem embellishes His crown.

Why do you think Hashem gets such pleasure from our תפילות?

What makes our עבודה so valuable to Him?

_____

_____

_____

_____

_____

_____

_____

הַמִּתְפַּלֵּל צָרִיךְ שֶׁיָּכִין מָקוֹם רָאוּי לִתְפִלָּתוֹ,
וְשֶׁיָּכִין לָה בְּגָדָיו וְגוּפוֹ וּמַחֲשַׁבְתּוֹ

(שלחן ערוך: סימן צ' סעיף א')

**A person should prepare a fit place to daven,
and should also prepare his clothing, body,
and thoughts for davening.**

*Why is it important to "prepare" yourself for
davening?*

_____

_____

_____

_____

_____

_____

_____

One of the students of the Baal Shem Tov once traveled to his Rebbe for יום כיפור. On the day before יום כיפור, since he didn't get to buy hay for the horses the day before, and they hadn't eaten the whole previous day, they needed to stand outside the city in the forest to graze.

In the middle of all this, the חסיד sat down to rest and fell asleep. When he got up he saw that the stars had already come out. Since he was far from the city, the חסיד was forced to remain outside the city and keep יום כיפור there. The חסיד was devastated about this, and he prayed in a heartbroken manner.

As soon as יום כיפור ended, the חסיד went back into the city to finally visit the Baal Shem Tov. The Baal Shem Tov received him with joy and said,**"You should know that your תפילות elevated all the תפילות of the 'people of the fields.'"**

How do you think the חסיד felt after the בעל שם טוב explained this to him?

An employee at a large, important company is invited to meet with the company president to ask for whatever he needs to better perform his job.

The employee barges in five minutes late, still checking his phone, after stopping to chat with a coworker.

He has things to do, so he quickly pulls out a paper with a list of things he wants and starts reading it out loud.

He then checks his phone one more time to see how much time this meeting has wasted.

Meanwhile, the company president sits and stares in shock, thinking, **"Why is this man wasting this precious opportunity?"**

Connect this story to davening.

_____

_____

_____

_____

_____

Q: The gragger has the handle on the bottom, while the dreidel is held from the top. Why is this so?

A: On Chanukah, Hashem saved us "from above": through a miracle.
On Purim, our salvation came about due to the merits of our own actions.
One of these actions was davening.
Davening is an effort we make. In turn, Hashem helps us out with things we need.

What do you need Hashem to help you with today?

_____

_____

_____

_____

When you daven today, relax knowing that you are doing your part. Hashem will take care of you.

פּוֹתֵחַ אֶת יָדֶךָ וּמַשְׂבִּיעַ לְכָל חַי רָצוֹן

You open Your hand and satisfy the
desire of every living being

While you are saying פותח, take advantage of
the moment to ask Hashem for whatever you
need.

One should have special concentration during
this phrase.

It is written in the שלחן ערוך that if one does not
have כוונה during this phrase, he should go back
and repeat it.

List four things Hashem provides for you.

1. _____

2. _____

3. _____

4. _____

וְאַתָּה נוֹתֵן לָהֶם אֶת אָכְלָם בְּעִתּוֹ

And You give them their food in its time

Q: What does it mean that Hashem gives food "בְּעִתּוֹ" — "in its time"?

A: The time Hashem chooses to give something is not always the time a person wants to receive something.

Hashem doesn't just give you *what* you need; He gives it to you *when* it is best for you to receive it.

What does the word "בְּעִתּוֹ" teach us?

_____

_____

_____

הַמַּאֲמִין בְּהַשְׁגָּחָה פְּרָטִית יוֹדֵעַ כִּי מֵהַשֵּׁם מִצְעֲדֵי
גֶבֶר כּוֹנָנוּ, אֲשֶׁר נְשָׁמָה זוֹ צְרִיכָה לְבָרֵר
וּלְתַקֵּן אֵיזֶה בֵּרוּר וְתִקּוּן בְּמָקוֹם פְּלוֹנִי

One who believes in השגחה פרטית knows that
"the steps of a person are made firm by
Hashem."

A person goes to a specific place because his
נשמה needs to refine and fix something there.
For hundreds of years, or even from the very
beginning of creation, the object that has to be
refined or perfected waits for that נשמה to come
do that task; and this נשמה itself, from the
moment of its creation, waits for the time to
come down to this world to refine/perfect that
which has been given to it.

*What is one positive thing you want to
accomplish today?*

_____

_____

*When you daven today, ask Hashem to
help you with it.*

Once, a villager came to town with an empty barrel to purchase wine. He went straight to the wine seller, who filled the barrel for him. Pleased, the villager whistled his way home. When he lifted the barrel, he was shocked to find that it wasn't heavy at all; in fact, it was empty! Furious, he returned all the way to the wine seller, shouting that he had been cheated. "I paid you a lot of money. How dare you give me an empty barrel?!"

The merchant was very confused. He was certain he'd filled the barrel to the brim. He said to him, "Let me take a look at your barrel. Maybe it leaked." Sure enough, there was a crack in the wood. The wine had seeped out slowly. The merchant then told his customer, "Next time you come to buy wine, make sure you bring a container capable of holding what you buy. Otherwise, you'll have no one to blame but yourself when you arrive home with an empty barrel."

Connect this story to davening.

_____

_____

Many people daven to Hashem that He should shower them with ברכות.

Often they do receive His ברכות, but they let them "slip through their fingers" by not being ready to receive them.

One should daven to become a strong vessel, worthy of containing Hashem's ברכות.

Every person has things they can work on. How will you ask Hashem to help you improve in your מידות? Choose an area and describe it in a few sentences.

A student in class is working hard on a math worksheet. While the rest of his classmates are wasting time, perhaps even complaining about it, this one student is taking the assignment seriously, concentrating, eyebrows furrowed as he struggles to solve the problems.
The teacher sees how hard his student his working, so he shortens the assignment and tells him he only has to complete half a page.

We must take the first step of working on ourselves.
In turn, Hashem will bless our efforts and actually make things easier for us!

Why does Hashem want us to put in this "beginning" effort?
Connect to davening.

_____

_____

_____

_____

_____

There are three categories in davening:

1. שבח: praising
2. בקשה: requesting
3. הודאה: thanking

Search through your סידור to find one תפילה for each category.

תפילה	CATEGORY
	שבח: Praising Hashem
	בקשה: Requesting for personal needs
	הודאה: Thanking Hashem, expressing gratitude

Make it personal! Talk to Hashem in your own words. Compose a short "text message" for each category.

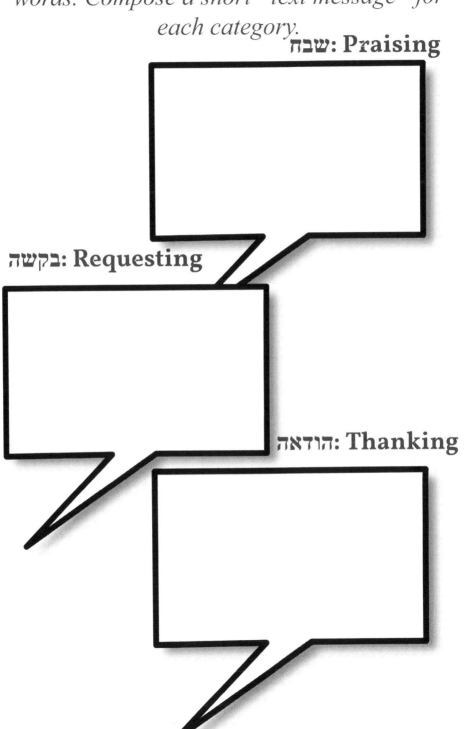

שבח: **Praising**

בקשה: **Requesting**

הודאה: **Thanking**

The חכמים have instituted ברכות קריאת שמע and יוצר אור, which are all about how the מלאכים are completely devoted to Hashem.

Q: Why are we talking about the מלאכים? It's their praise, not ours.

A: We look to the holy מלאכים, so that we can emulate their ways. This helps us awaken our own love for Hashem!

What is the difference between a human being and a מלאך?

_____

_____

We aren't expected to be מלאכים — but what can we learn from them to inspire us in our davening?

_____

_____

_____

We say "קָדוֹשׁ" as a way to remind ourselves of how glorious and separated Hashem is from us. But we also know that Hashem is everywhere.

Q: How can we simultaneously believe that:
a) Hashem is distanced and separated,

and

b) Hashem is found in every place?

A: Hashem *is* everywhere, but not in a revealed way. We can't see Him all the time.

Why? A level of separation is important for the king-subject relationship.

Imagine if a king would reveal himself completely to his nation. He'd take people on tours of his private living quarters, and chat with them in the streets all the time. It might be exciting at first, but then the people would lose their respect for him.

By announcing "קָדוֹשׁ" in davening, we proclaim our awe and respect for Hashem.

Which sections in davening remind us to have awe and respect?

When a friend is expecting you to call, all you need to do is dial a number. **So too, Hashem is waiting for us to "dial His number" — to daven — and He will answer us.**

In the phone below, write what you plan to "discuss" with Hashem today when you daven!

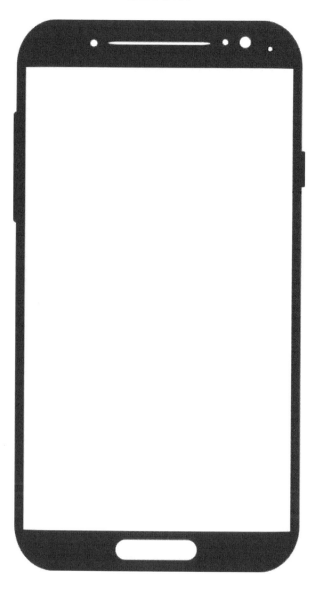

When יעקב davened to Hashem to save him from עשו, he said:

"קטנתי מכל החסדים"

"I have become small from all the kindnesses"

(וישלח 32:11)

The Alter Rebbe explains in תניא that this means:

"שבכל חסד וחסד שהקדוש ברוך הוא עושה לאדם, צריך להיות שפל רוח במאוד"

"That with every single favor that Hashem grants a person, one needs to become very humble."

(אגרת הקדש : ב)

When we realize how much goodness Hashem grants us, it causes us to feel "small" (humble). This enables us to daven with even greater passion.

Why do you think it is important to be humble when davening?

_____

_____

Have you ever wanted to look at the sun but then had to turn your face away because the light was too bright?

The מלאכים are on such a high level that they swing between two states: אהבה, love, and יראה, fear. They go close to Hashem from an intense desire to be near Him, and then they retreat far when it's too much holiness to withstand.

This is called "רצוא ושוב" — drawing close, and retreating. Hashem hides Himself so that we don't get 'blinded' by His intense light. But at the same time, He wants us to get to know Him, learning on a level we can understand.

Describe how this connects to davening.

_____

_____

_____

_____

_____

The service of a person is somewhat similar to the מלאכים.

We need to be in a state of **רצוא** — to break away from our worldly boundaries so that we can unite with our Source above.

We also need to be in a state of **שוב** — with feet firmly planted in this physical world — doing what Hashem wants us to do here.

מצוות cannot be done by the מלאכים. They can only be done here, by us, in the physical world.

Davening is a time to connect to the higher worlds. It's a time to recharge.

After davening, we go into the world and fulfill our mission with that energy.

How does davening help you "recharge"? What thoughts can you have in mind to make the most of the time?

_____

_____

_____

_____

The Manager's Mistake

Once there was a boss who went on vacation, so he put a manager in charge in his place. All the workers were instructed to report to the manager's office every day and listen to him reading the instructions. Every day, he called all the workers to his office and read the instructions out loud, just as he was told to do. But when the boss returned, he was shocked to see the condition of his factory. Machines were broken. Workers stood around, snacking and chatting. The boss angrily asked the manager for an explanation. "Did you follow the instructions I left behind with you?" "Of course!" the manager said. "I read them to all the workers every day while you were gone." "Now I know why this place is a mess!" the boss said. "You read the instructions, but you didn't care to see that they were actually fulfilled. Do you think I left them for you as reading material? **I expected them to be read so that they would be carried out!**"

Connect to davening.

"מלך עוזר ומושיע ומגן"
"King, Helper, Savior, and Shield"

These four adjectives describe Hashem's relationship with us.

מלך: Hashem is a gracious King and we are His subjects.

עוזר: When we address Hashem as "Helper", this is closer than a king. A helper is someone we can call on in a time of need.

מושיע: "Savior" represents a closer relationship where Hashem is available to rescue us in an instant without the need to call on Him.

מגן: Finally, a "Shield" suggests that Hashem is so close that He surrounds us like a suit of armor so that nothing in the world can come to harm us.

Why do you think Hashem relates to us in these different levels? Why not just one?

_____

_____

הַיוֹם יוֹם: כ"ו תמוז

אִין לֶערנֶען תּוֹרָה פִּילט זִיךְ אַ אִיד וְוי
אַ תַּלְמִיד בַּא אַ רֶבִּי'ן, אִין דאַוְונֶען —
וְוי אַ קִינד בַּא אַ פֿאָטֶער.

When a person studies תורה, he focuses on his understanding. During davening, he is connecting to Hashem in a way that is HIGHER than understanding.

When learning תורה the Jew feels like a student with his teacher; in davening - like a child with his father.

How does davening bring out the feelings of a parent-child relationship within us? Describe.

Someone once asked the Chofetz Chaim whether it wouldn't be better to wait to daven when one is inspired, rather than to say the תפילות without any כוונה. The Chofetz Chaim answered with a משל: Many towns and villages couldn't afford their own watchmaker, so a repairman would travel between the villages. When he'd arrive, he'd sit down and sort the broken watches into two piles: the watches that could be fixed, and those which were beyond repair. The watches that had been regularly wound by their owners could easily be fixed. But the watches that had become rusted from not being used for a long time went into the second pile. **The Chofetz Chaim said that if you daven each day, even if you daven without כוונה, at least the davening tools are well oiled.** But a person who doesn't daven loses the habit and won't be able to daven easily, even when inspired.

Why weren't some watches able to be repaired?

_____

_____

_____

A woman once took some baskets of apples to the market to sell. Some children knocked over her baskets, scattering the apples all over the place.

She stood there, devastated, watching as the children grabbed her apples and ran away.

Finally a person standing nearby suggested, **"Why don't you take some of the apples yourself?"**

It's important to keep davening, even if one is not in the mood. Then, there is at least a chance that some תפילות will be said with some concentration. If one doesn't try at all, they won't have that chance to begin with.

Why is it important to daven even if not in the mood?

_____

_____

_____

If one feels they are unable to daven properly, they should seek to strengthen themselves and do what they can.

For even when they cannot express themselves well, their words are still precious to Hashem.

This is the meaning of the words:

"הֲבֵן יַקִּיר לִי אֶפְרַיִם אִם יֶלֶד שַׁעֲשֻׁעִים"

(ירמיהו ל"א:י"ט)

"...Ephraim my beloved son, a child I cherish"

Even though very young children cannot speak properly and can only make signs, using broken words, their parents still delight in such communication and seek to fulfill their requests.

Why is our davening precious to Hashem even if it isn't perfect?

_____

_____

_____

_____

In תפילת שחרית we say Hashem's Name close to
six hundred times!

Each time we say Hashem's name, we should
try to improve our כוונה, and keep in mind that
he is "היה, הווה, ויהיה" — "was, is, and will be"
forever.

Look through your סידור.

*Color in a square for each time you find
Hashem's Name!*

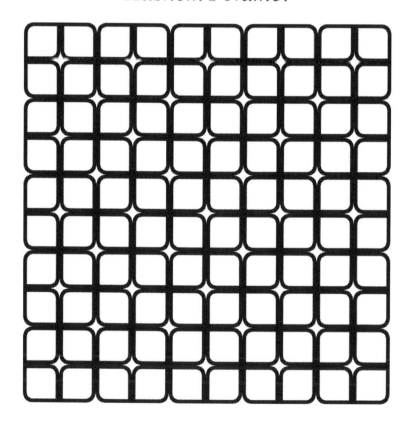

When the Chasam Sofer was asked why he took so much time davening when he could be spending that time learning תורה, he replied that whoever takes his time davening is granted longer life, so he would therefore have enough time left to learn more.

You might be tempted to daven quickly because you might be worried that you won't have time to do other things.

But know that when you daven slowly, Hashem will provide you with the time and energy you need to complete your tasks!

What can you tell yourself today to motivate yourself to daven slowly?

_____

_____

_____

_____

_____

Even healthy people must daven for health, and rich people for wealth, because no one has any way of knowing what the future holds.

Write down a list of five things you always had in the past (and hope you'll always have).

1. _____

2. _____

3. _____

4. _____

5. _____

Today, daven to Hashem to continue to provide you with the things you take for granted.

Although rain is necessary, do people
remember to ask for it every day?
Would a lawyer on the way to work remember
to ask Hashem for health?
Would a doctor remember to ask for wisdom?

We need all these things, but it's easy to forget
to ask for these necessities when we are caught
up in the hustle of life.

This is why it is important to follow the text of
the סידור.

**Our חכמים created a set system for davening
which includes all of a person's
requirements, in order to ensure that we will
always daven for everything we need.**

*Look inside שמונה עשרה and write down the
תפילות for wisdom and health.*

"ה' שפתי תפתח ופי יגיד תהילתך"

"Hashem, open my lips and allow my mouth to tell your praise…"

We begin שמונה עשרה with the plea that Hashem should open our lips and help our mouths tell His true praise. We ask Hashem to help us express ourselves properly when we daven.

Why might a person not be able to express themselves properly during davening? How can they overcome this blockage?

_____

_____

_____

_____

_____

Hashem is both our Father and our King.

We relate differently to each.

Describe a king in five words:

_____

_____

_____

_____

_____

Describe a father in five words:

_____

_____

_____

_____

_____

Hashem listens to all our תפילות. Sometimes the answer is "yes", sometimes the answer is "not now", and sometimes the answer is "no, because there is something better in store for you".

Give an example of a request someone might make, and how there might be different reasons for their תפילה not being fulfilled.
You can share a real situation or create a story.

_____

_____

_____

_____

_____

_____

_____

_____

_____

When a person pronounces each word carefully, using the letters of the Aleph Beis properly, all of creation becomes partners with him.

The song of a passing bird may join in his תפילה, reaching the heavens.

Why do you think it is important to make an effort to pronounce the words carefully?

_____

_____

_____

_____

When Rabbi Eliezer of Volozhin saw a student who davened quickly, he called him in to speak about the importance of davening slowly and with concentration.

"But Rebbe, let me explain myself," said the student. "Imagine a man who is traveling by wagon. If the wagon goes too slowly, all types of creatures jump onto it. If the wagon travels very fast, however, nothing can jump on. Similarly, when I daven slowly, all types of thoughts can distract me, but when I daven quickly I don't have that problem."

"I'm afraid, however," replied R' Eliezer Yitzchok, "That when you daven as fast as you do, YOU may be one of the 'creatures' that doesn't manage to jump onto the wagon."

~

It's better to daven slowly than to rush, even if you don't have perfect כוונה. **Today, give yourself time to slow down so you can "jump onto the wagon".**

Which תפילה will you read slowly today?

וְכִי תָבֹאוּ מִלְחָמָה בְּאַרְצְכֶם עַל הַצַּר הַצֹּרֵר אֶתְכֶם וַהֲרֵעֹתֶם בַּחֲצֹצְרֹת וַנְזְכַּרְתֶּם לִפְנֵי ה' אֱלֹקיכֶם וְנוֹשַׁעְתֶּם מֵאֹיְבֵיכֶם

(במדבר י:ט)

And when you go to war in your land against your enemies that are causing you to suffer, you should blow the Shofar with your trumpets and be remembered before Hashem, and you will be saved from your enemies

In a time of distress, the מצוה of תפילה is דאורייתא — it is required by the תורה.

In moments of pain, we need to recognize that Hashem is our only salvation.

Why do you think it is important to daven during a time of distress instead of just relying on yourself?

_____

_____

_____

_____

The בעל שם טוב tells us of a great king who once announced that any requests brought to him would be granted.

Many people came with their requests, some asking for gold and silver, others for high positions.

But there was one wise man who made a very different request. He asked the king if he could have permission to meet with him three times each day. The king was very pleased with this request, seeing that this man cared more about speaking with the king even more than gold and riches.

He told the man that whenever he'd come, he would be allowed to go into the treasure room and take anything he wanted.

Today during davening, think about the fact that being able to speak to Hashem is a privilege.

Why was the king happier with the wise man's request than he was with everyone else's?

_____

_____

וַעֲבַדְתֶּם אֵת ה' אֱלֹקיכֶם
וּבֵרַךְ אֶת־לַחְמְךָ וְאֶת־מֵימֶיךָ
(שמות כג:כה)

And you will serve Hashem
and He will bless your bread and your water

It is a מצוה מן התורה to ask Hashem for whatever
one might need.

The פסוק above teaches us that we must daven
to ask Hashem for our needs every day. Just as
bread and water are daily necessities, so is
תפילה a daily obligation.

Why do you think Hashem wants us to turn to
Him whenever we need something?

_____

_____

_____

_____

_____

Once there was a small bird that fell out of its nest and landed near a lion.
Terrified, it cried out, "Hashem, help me!"
So Hashem said, "I will give you wings."
When the bird discovered two heavy things hanging on his sides, he was even more terrified! He begged, "Hashem, please remove my wings! They are so heavy! Now I can't outrun the lion!"
Hashem answered him, "Yes they are heavy. But these wings will take you far above and beyond what any other animal can do."

Serving Hashem is a responsibility. Learning תורה and doing מצוות requires a lot of concentration. But don't be foolish like the bird; **these responsibilities are not "heavy things". They are tools to help you soar!**

Connect this story to davening.

_____

_____

_____

_____

It states in תניא that "אהבה", love, and "יראה", awe, are the two "wings" that help a person's תורה and מצוות soar to שמים.

Draw two wings! Inside each wing, write some words about what it feels like to love Hashem, and what it feels like to be in awe of Him.

The בעל שם טוב visited a town in which the people complained that their חזן sang "על חטא" in a happy tune, rather than in a more serious one. When the בעל שם טוב asked him why he did this, the חזן explained: "Rebbe, a king has many servants. Some of them prepare the royal meals, others guard the gates, and still others are in charge of the documents. Each of them takes pleasure in being able to work for the king.

"There's also a janitor in charge of cleaning the palace. Is he depressed because he is looking at dirt all day? No! He's happy, because he is also serving the king. He's not thinking about the dirt. He's thinking about making the palace beautiful. When a Jew sins, he has 'dirt' on his נשמה. When he is confessing in "על חטא" it's not the עבירות that he's thinking about, but the קדושה and beauty of his נשמה. **Is that not a reason to rejoice?"**

When in davening do we ask Hashem to forgive us for our עבירות?

Q:

Sometimes people wonder, "Why isn't it enough to just *think* a תפילה?

Why do we have to verbalize our davening?

A:

Speaking creates a certain level of clarity — not just for the listeners, but for the speakers themselves.

When we are required to express our thoughts and desires through words, we understand those thoughts and desires better!

Why do we have to say the words when we daven?

_____

_____

_____

_____

אַךְ עֵת וּזְמַן הַחִיזּוּק וְאִימּוּץ הַזְּרוֹעוֹת וְהָרֹאשׁ הִיא שְׁעַת תְּפִלַּת הַשַּׁחַר

The time for strengthening the spiritual emotions and intellect is the time of davening in the morning,

שֶׁהִיא שְׁעַת רַחֲמִים וְעֵת רָצוֹן הָעֶלְיוֹן לְמַעְלָה

for Above, that is a time of compassion, a time at which Hashem's Will is revealed.

The time of davening is a time of great compassion. Hashem has mercy on us and makes it easier for us to work on our מידות.

When was a time you felt Hashem's compassion? (Think of a difficult situation that got better!)

_____

_____

_____

_____

In שמונה עשרה, the opening section begins with:
"אלקי אברהם, אלקי יצחק, ואלקי יעקב"

Each of the אבות represent a different way of serving Hashem.

Kindness	חסד	אברהם
Strength, discipline	גבורה	יצחק
Compassion, balance	תפארת	יעקב

We see from this that there is no "one-size-fits-all" when it comes to how we connect with Hashem. While we all have the same תורה and מצוות, we each have a unique "flavor" in how we fulfill it.

Why do you think it is important to remember this as we begin שמונה עשרה?

_____

_____

_____

It says in תניא that even if one has thought about the meaning of each part of davening only once throughout the entire year, **that is enough to elevate all the תפילות of the year.**

One perfect תפילה lifts up all your other תפילות for the year!

Draw a picture of תפילות being lifted by the words of one תפילה you will concentrate on today more than you usually do.

We need to daven perfectly in thought, speech, and action.

However, Hashem knows we are not perfect and will make mistakes.

Therefore, Hashem sends the מלאכים to go around and listen to our davening each day. Each day the מלאכים collect words that were said with כוונה. They piece together a word here, a תפילה there, so that every ראש השנה, a complete, perfect davening will be presented to Hashem!

Which תפילה would you like to focus on with perfect כוונה today?

_____

_____

What can you tell yourself to make it easier to focus on it?   ·

_____

_____

_____

Q: Why can't we daven to Hashem in our own words? Why do we have to daven from a סידור with set תפילות?

A: People actually used to daven this way. They would wake up in the morning and immediately turn to Hashem to praise, thank, and ask for what they needed, sometimes several times per day. But as time passed, people didn't know how to word their requests. Some people would talk to Hashem very little, and some wouldn't turn to Him at all.

Therefore, חז"ל instituted a basic text for everyone to follow and be able to fulfill the הלכה of davening to Hashem each day.

The words of the סידור are holy. Even if we don't understand every word, if we daven with pure intention, Hashem will accept our תפילות.

Why did חז"ל set up the סידור?

_____

_____

The Baal Shem Tov would encourage people to say words of praise to Hashem in their own language and constantly say phrases like "ברוך ה'" and "בעזרת ה'".

He revealed that these simple words accomplish more than the mystical כוונות of the מקובלים.

Why do you think it is important to have BOTH the pre-set framework of the סידור (as discussed on the previous page) as well as our own personal תפילות that come from our heart? Why can't it just be one or the other?

_____

_____

_____

_____

_____

_____

An actor knows that it's important to say the words exactly as they appear in the script. He can't say whatever he wants on the stage. However, the audience will notice when an actor is just reading the lines without any thought as to what he is saying.

An actor who deeply understands and feels excited about his part will make a lasting impression. It's all about the emotion!

It's important to learn the translations so that you can insert your own "כוונות" — your own thoughts and feelings. This way, the תפילות will feel like your own.

Go through your סידור, and pick <u>one line</u> which you would like to know the translation of, and write it down below. (Ask your teacher to help you translate it.)

_____

_____

_____

_____

_____

Ever wondered why you sometimes *'shuckel'* (sway) while you daven?

That's because the יחידה, the core of the נשמה, shines during davening like the flame of a candle. Davening time is like a refreshing cup of water for the thirsty נשמה that desperately wants to connect with Hashem! You are doing a huge favor for your נפש אלוקית when you put aside all your daily tasks to focus only on Hashem for this period of time. Your נשמה gets so excited, and that's why it subconsciously causes your body to sway!

This state of excitement is called "דביקות", when your נשמה feels so close to Hashem that it's overwhelming. Any Jew can reach this state. Of course, it takes patience and practice to be able to focus completely on your נשמה and ignore all other distractions.

What does closeness to Hashem feel like for you, physically and emotionally?

_____

_____

_____

Once there were two neighbors. They lived in a forest far away from any lakes or rivers. In order to collect water, they needed to put out barrels and wait for rain to fall to fill it up. Each man had a different approach.

One would keep his barrels in his house. He'd wake up early each morning to scan the horizon, and if he saw clouds, he would put out the barrels. Then he would take them back inside after it rained, and if he saw it starting to drizzle again, he would run back outside to put them out.

The other man had his barrels out all the time, no matter the weather. He left them in his yard all day and all night, even if the skies were clear and no rain was in sight.

Who do you think collected more rainwater in the end? Why?

_____

_____

_____

_____

In the story on the previous page, the second man collected more rainwater — because his barrels were out 24/7. He was able to catch every drop. If it ever drizzled or poured in the middle of the night unexpectedly, he was prepared.

Similarly, Hashem has plenty of ברכות in store. He is waiting for you to reach out and ask!

If you daven only whenever you feel like it, you may be missing out on opportunities. When you daven every single day, you will collect many ברכות!

In the raindrops, write down some ברכות you would like to collect!

The students of Rabbi Shimon bar Yochai asked him why the Mann had to fall every day; why didn't Hashem give it to them as a yearly supply?

He answered with a משל: The king's only son, whom the king loved dearly, visited his father once a year to collect his allowance. Wanting to see his son more often, the king decided that he would stop giving the money once a year. The son would have to come each day to the palace to collect it. Through this arrangement, the king was then able to have the pleasure of his son's company each and every day. So too, Hashem wanted to hear from the Jews every single day, and so He gave just one day's portion of Mann at a time so that they would ask for it more often.

In turning to Hashem with our daily תפילות, we bring Hashem great pleasure.

Why did Hashem make the Mann fall daily instead of yearly?

_____

_____

_____

When two people embrace, there is no space between them — and no time needs to pass for them to talk to each other. They are already as close as can be!

When a person is completely one with Hashem, his תפילה will be answered immediately.

What thoughts and actions would help you feel "one" with Hashem?

_____

_____

_____

_____

_____

_____

_____

_____

As the Alter Rebbe neared the end of his life, he looked up at the ceiling and asked his grandson, "What do you see?"

"I see a beam."

The Alter Rebbe responded, "And *I* see דבר ה', the word of Hashem, ורוח פיו, and the spirit of His mouth, that gives life to that beam and allows it to continue to exist..."

Feel your pulse. Breathe in and out. Look at your hands, blink your eyes, smile.

YOU EXIST!

Marvel on the fact that Hashem is commanding YOU to be here right now.

What is something special that you can contribute to the world TODAY?

_____

_____

_____

When you take three steps back and three steps forward in שמונה עשרה, imagine yourself facing the כותל.

Write a note that you would put it in the כותל.

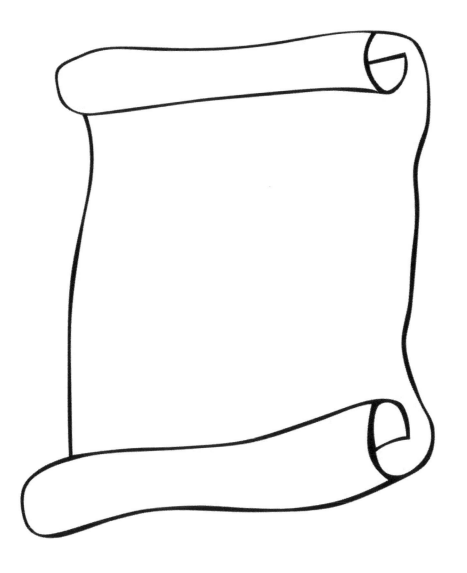

Q: Why, when we daven, do we ask for material blessings like health and wealth? Shouldn't we only daven to Hashem for spiritual concerns?

A: We can't serve Hashem properly if we're worried about physical problems.

We ask Hashem to bless us with good health and livelihood so that we can serve Him fully!

This is like a servant asking his master for tools to help him work faster.

Write a list of 5 things that help you serve Hashem.

1. _____

2. _____

3. _____

4. _____

5. _____

When משה asked to enter ארץ ישראל, he could have relied on his merits.

But from the word "ואתחנן", we learn that משה "pleaded" — he asked Hashem for it as a free gift, as a favor.

Why do you think משה asked for the privilege to enter ארץ ישראל as a "gift", even though he could have said he rightfully deserved it?

_____

_____

_____

"אני בצדק אחזה פניך"

"Through צדקה I will grasp Your face"

Hashem says that when we give צדקה, He will "receive our face" (accept our תפילות).
By giving צדקה in the morning before davening, (and thus giving a poor person life), our own תפילות come alive.

Rabbi Eliezer would give a poor man צדקה every morning before davening for this reason.

What do you think it means for תפילות to come "alive"? What would that davening experience feel like?

_____

_____

_____

_____

_____

The miracle of פורים teaches us that even after a decree has been finalized in שמים, sincere תשובה and תפילה can change that decree. When the Jews heard what was being planned against them, they fasted and davened.

How do you think the Jews felt when they heard about the decree against them? Write a diary entry as if you were a young child living through this moment in history. Describe the davening experience.

_____

_____

_____

_____

_____

_____

_____

_____

_____

עבודת התפלה

Q: Davening is referred to as "work". What work is required of us?

A: Hundreds of thoughts pass through our mind in just a short amount of time. As we daven, many of these random thoughts come to disturb us.

The effort to ignore these thoughts and focus on davening is the work required of us, since it is not easy.

Why do you think these thoughts come to disturb us specifically during davening?

_____

_____

_____

_____

_____

A חסיד once came to the Maggid of Mezeritch with a question. "I know we can serve Hashem with our actions. But how are we supposed to control our thoughts?" Instead of answering, the Maggid told him to go to Zhitomir. "Go visit my חסיד, R' Zev," he said. "He can help you." So the חסיד embarked on the trip. It was a long journey through the Russian winter. He traveled for weeks. When he finally arrived in the town, he saw a window filled with light. Through it, he saw R' Zev bent over his ספרים. The חסיד knocked, but R' Zev didn't get up to answer. He knocked again. For hours he stood in the freezing cold until finally, R' Zev got up to answer. He greeted him and prepared a warm cup of tea. For a few days the חסיד enjoyed R' Zev's hospitality. He finally felt ready to ask him the question: "How are we expected to control our thoughts?"

"Ah," R' Zev answered. "Is a man any less a master of his own self than he is of his home? I gave you my answer on the night you arrived. In my home, I'm the boss. Those I wish to invite, I allow in; those I do not wish to admit, I do not."

Underline the lesson the חסיד learned.

If a thought comes your way, **you have the choice** whether or not to allow yourself to be distracted by it.

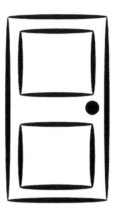

Write a few techniques you can use to push away distracting thoughts.

If you have never exercised in your life, you will need to begin in slow increments. Gradually, you can build up you strength and add more to your routine.

When davening, it is good to improve in slow stages. Don't exhaust all your strength at the very beginning. Strengthen yourself bit by bit.

Challenge yourself by adding a תפילה every week or a new line every day.

Write about a time you had to challenge yourself. How did you build up your strength? Share how you can carry the lessons from that experience over to davening.

_____

_____

_____

_____

A plane taking off on the runway begins its journey on the ground; but it soon rises above the clouds and soars through clear skies.

When you begin to daven, you may find yourself surrounded by noise. You may have worries, thoughts, and plans for the day. **But as soon as you begin davening, you feel like a weight has lifted off of your shoulders. In your heart, you will feel relaxed.**

Draw what a calm place looks like for you. During davening, keep yourself centered by visualizing yourself in this space.

There are מלאכים who praise Hashem once every seven years. According to some, it is only once every 50 years.

When they do sing their praises, some say one word: "קדוש"; others say "ברוך"; and others, one full פסוק.

If you could only praise Hashem once every 50 years, what would you say? Write it down below.

_____

_____

_____

_____

_____

_____

We, בני ישראל, are privileged to be able to praise Hashem at any time of day, for however long we want.

From רש"י (in בראשית מח:יא) we learn that the word "להתפלל", "to daven", also means "to think".

Davening is a set time for us to *think* about spiritual matters.

Material matters can occupy our full attention during the day.

We have to push these thoughts away during davening time so that we can focus on Hashem.

How does focusing on Hashem in the morning give us energy for the rest of the day?

_____

_____

_____

_____

_____

_____

Dancing in a Prison Cell: (Part 1)

Two brothers, R' Elimelech of Lizensk and R' Zushe of Anipoli, were once arrested.

They sat quietly in their prison cell, knowing that they were innocent and hoping they would soon be released.

After a few hours passed, R' Elimelech stood up to daven מנחה.

"What are you doing?" his brother asked.

"I'm getting ready for מנחה," replied R' Elimelech.

R' Zushe responded, "We aren't allowed to daven in this cell because there is a pail here, and one is not permitted to daven in a room with a toilet."

Disappointed, R' Elimelech sat down and began to cry. "Why are you crying?" asked R' Zushe. "Is it because you can't daven?"

"Yes." R' Elimelech responded.

Why was R' Elimelech not allowed to daven?

_____

_____

_____

Dancing in a Prison Cell: (Part 2)

"But why cry?" R' Zushe asked his brother. "Don't you know that the same Hashem who commanded you to daven, also commanded you not to daven when the room is unfit? By *not* davening in this room, you're fulfilling Hashem's will, even if it doesn't feel right."

"My brother, that is true!" R' Elimelech exclaimed, a smile spreading across his face. He took his brother's arm and began to dance in joy. The guards heard the celebration and came running. Watching the two brothers dancing, the guards asked the other prisoners what had occurred. "We have no idea!" they said. "Those two Jews were talking about the pail in the corner and then they began to dance." "They're happy because of the pail?" the guards smirked. "Okay, we'll take away the pail if that is their reason to dance!" They took out the pail from the cell. The brothers were then able to daven!

Why do you think Hashem rewarded the brothers with the ability to daven?

During the Russian Civil War, the Alter of Slabodka was davening in a room, when heavy bombing began.

While he and his מנין were in the middle of שמונה עשרה, a large chandelier came crashing down from the ceiling.

After finishing his davening, the Alter saw the chandelier on the floor and turned to ask how it had come to be there.

He had been concentrating so deeply in his תפילה that he didn't notice it crashing down to the floor!

What do you learn from this story?
How can you apply this in your own davening?

_____

_____

_____

_____

_____

_____

The בעל שם טוב related that a very harsh decree had been proclaimed in שמים. The צדיקים were not able to cancel his decree, even with their most intense תפילות.

A woman, upon hearing the congregation's desperate cries, begged of Hashem:

"רבונו של עולם! How can You not accept the pleas of Your children? I am only a human being, and I don't have endless patience. Yet when any of my children cry, it pierces my heart, and I would do anything to stop their tears. But You are infinite and Your compassion is unlimited. Listen how all Your children are crying. You must help them and relieve their pain!"

"What we were not able to do," recounted the בעל שם טוב, "was accomplished by this righteous woman. It was her simple but heartfelt תפילה that caused Hashem to nullify the decree."

Why do you think the woman was able to overturn the decree when even the צדיקים were not able to?

People generally recognize their king. But when the king goes out to war, he disguises himself. At such a time, only his most trusted officials know where he is.

There is one way, though, that even regular citizens can locate him. All they need to do is look for where there is a high concentration of security — that is where the king can be found!

The בעל שם טוב explains that when an individual prepares himself to daven, the יצר הרע immediately tries to come and disturb his concentration. A person must know, however, that the obstacle that he faces clearly shows that this is where the King is found! **The fact that כוונה is so hard shows that "security" for the King is strongest there.** Hashem is close to all who call upon Him. In such a situation, one must daven even harder to overcome the hurdles and reach the King.

Why does the יצר הרע come to disturb us during davening?

_____

_____

Singing can bring you greater excitement and feeling.

Using a tune when you daven is a great way to help you make sure you are saying the words with joy.

Many people associate memories with songs. Do you have any memories of a specific song or tune being sung in davening (in shul, or anywhere else)? Write about the feelings it brings up in you.

_____

_____

_____

_____

_____

Rav Shimon Sofer was the Rav in a Hungarian town. The Hungarian emperor arranged a visit to the town.

Rav Sofer planned to say the ברכה one must say when in the presence of a king.

The הלכה is to say a ברכה from a paper if one is not familiar with it — so he wrote it down.

When he neared the king and began saying the ברכה, he was so overcome with awe and nervousness that he dropped the paper. He said the ברכה by heart.

That night in Shul, Rav Sofer started to weep. Someone asked him why he was crying.

Rav Sofer said, **"I am crying because although I dropped the paper while speaking to a human king, I didn't drop my סידור when speaking to Hashem…"**

What did Rav Sofer mean by that?

_____

_____

_____

_____

A boat out at sea had one Jewish child aboard. Deep into the voyage, a ferocious storm descended upon them. Howling winds and torrential rain pummeled their ship. In desperation, the non-Jewish passengers turned to their idols and cried out to them. Realizing that their idols couldn't help them, they said to the Jewish child, "Call out to your G-d, for we have heard that He answers you when you cry out to him, and that He is strong." **The child began to daven with all his heart. Hashem accepted his תפילות. The storm disappeared, and the sea became still and calm.**

What do you think this child felt while davening?

_____

_____

_____

There once was a simple villager who was unable to read. Whenever he'd receive a letter, he would ask the local מלמד to read it to him.

One day he received a letter carrying the unfortunate news that his father had passed away. Upon hearing this from the מלמד (who was reading the letter), the villager fainted on the spot.

Later on, people asked the מלמד why he didn't faint as well. "After all," they said, "It was you who was actually reading the letter!"

"The letter wasn't about *my* father," the מלמד replied. "It was about *his* father!"

~~~

Davening is a time to recognize that Hashem is real and relevant to our lives. When we absorb this knowledge, it will affect us in a deeper way.

What can you tell yourself today to make davening feel relevant?

Imagine yourself about to enter the palace of the King for a special celebration.
As you walk up the beautiful path to the grand golden gates, enemies suddenly come and block your path.

Connect to davening.

_____

_____

_____

_____

_____

_____

_____

_____

_____

_____

In the city of Krasna, a man announced that he would walk across the river on a tightrope if he was given 100 gold coins.

R' Chaim of Krasna came to watch. He was impressed at the man's ability to concentrate.

Afterwards, R' Chaim remarked to his students, **"If for 100 gold coins a person can focus so well on what he's doing, how much more so should we concentrate when davening to Hashem!"**

What do we gain from davening that's better than 100 gold coins? Share below.

_____

_____

_____

As you daven, try to form a mental image of the words you are saying in your mind.

When you picture the letters this way, you will be able to focus better, and your תפילות will go straight to שמים.

Draw the word "שמע" in a beautiful way to imprint the word in your mind.

Once, an entire nation was invited to greet a king on his birthday. His officials and advisors brought him gifts, some bearing platters of delectable sweets, others carrying expensive cuts of meat. There was a simple farmer who also wished to show his love, but he didn't have the means to do so extravagantly as the others did. Still, he dressed in his finest clothing and cut the choicest stalks of grain from his wheat field. When it was his turn to greet the king, he pulled out the bundle from his sack and said, "Your Majesty, I want to honor you just as everyone else. However, this is the best I can give you. Please take my grain and give it to your chefs to bake what pleases you."

Every day, we daven to Hashem with our very best effort. Still, we know we are not on a level to have perfect כוונה. **Nevertheless, we present our תפילות to Hashem with a whole heart and hope that He will accept them as fitting.**

Why do you think the king loved the farmer's gift even though it was simple?

A young child wanted to get a gumball from a machine in a store. She put in a quarter and turned it, but nothing happened.
She tried again but still, there was no result. She twisted it one more time. To her disappointment, nothing happened. Frustrated, she asked a store employee to help her out. The worker opened the cover to see what was blocking it. Peering inside, they discovered an extra gumball wedged in there. To their surprise, when they pulled it out, three gumballs came tumbling out. The child got to keep all of them!

Sometimes you daven and daven and don't see the result. That doesn't mean that Hashem isn't listening, חס ושלום, He is collecting all of your **תפילות! You will receive the accumulated ברכות when the right time comes, and they might be even better than you had originally imagined!**

What is something you are waiting for?

"וְהִנֵּה סֻלָּם מֻצָּב אַרְצָה"

הַיּוֹם יוֹם ה' כִּסְלֵו

תְּפִלָּה הִיא סֻלָּם הַהִתְקַשְּׁרוּת שֶׁל הַנְּשָׁמָה בֶּאלֹקוּת

"Davening is the ladder which connects the נשמה to Hashem"

The ladder is situated on the ground. Davening "stands on the ground", beginning with words of thanks, yet "וראשו מגיע השמימה": its top reaches towards שמים (a state in which one is only thinking about Hashem).

One gets to this level by understanding and thinking about the פסוקי דזמרה, ברכות קריאת שמע and קריאת שמע.

What is the first פסוקי דזמרה of תפילה?

_____

_____

The Baal Shem Tov was once traveling with some of his students during the winter. Passing over a frozen river, they noticed some villagers carving out the image of their עבודה זרה in the ice.

The Baal Shem Tov ordered the wagon to stop so they could all stay and watch them work.

The students were startled. Why had they stopped to watch such a scene? One of them finally worked up the courage to ask.

The Baal Shem Tov answered:

"Everything one sees and hears must be a lesson for his עבודת ה'. The villagers were only able to carve out the shape of their עבודה זרה in the river because it was frozen."

From this we learn that in order to avoid having negative things make an impression on us, we must fill our lives with the warmth and excitement of קדושה.

How can you get yourself excited about Hashem?

_____

_____

"אשרי יושבי ביתך **עוד** יהללוך סלה"

(*Fortunate are the dwellers of Your house,
who **still** praise You continuously*)

Fortunate are people who can STILL thank
Hashem even when things don't appear good
at the moment.

Constantly thanking Hashem trains us to
recognize how everything is good!

**One who says אשרי three times each day is
guaranteed a place in עולם הבא,** because a
person who lives with the above mentality is
guaranteed to feel this closeness with Hashem
forever — in this world and the next — like a
"dweller" in His house.

*Why is it important to thank Hashem even
when we don't understand His ways?*

_____

_____

_____

Just as songs have choruses that repeat, so too there are many themes and ideas that are repeated within תפילות.

The purpose of this is to instill a mood. Just as a song is more powerful when the chorus repeats itself, so too we daven and praise Hashem numerous times so that the message can become a part of us.

Often, one needs to hear or say something more than once for it to have an effect.

Find תפילות that make you feel the following emotions:

Grateful	
Excited	
Serious	
Special	

ובטובו מחדש בכל יום תמיד מעשה בראשית

In Hashem's goodness, He renews each day the works of creation

Every moment, Hashem constantly chooses to give life to His creations.

Without this renewal, everything would simply disappear!

Write a list of 4 things you hope will continue to exist today for you.

1. _____
2. _____
3. _____
4. _____

Review this list before you begin davening and think about how Hashem is choosing to make these things exist, just for you!

Today, imagine you are the main actor in your davening "play". Describe how the "props" and "scene" should look. Describe your "lines", who your "Audience" is, and what is expected of you!

Imagine if a stranger would come right up to you and command you, "You must love me." You might feel confused. It would be pretty hard to love a stranger.

But imagine that "stranger" is actually someone who, apparently, knows you from when you were a child. For years, the "stranger" has been providing you with money, sending you gifts, and hiring the very best doctors to care for your health — all without you realizing.

If you knew this information, you might be overwhelmed with love!

This is how you should view your relationship with Hashem — but with one exception: Hashem is not a stranger. He created you!

Meditating on this idea can bring you to feel deep love towards Hashem.

Which תפילה commands you to "love Hashem with all your heart"?

Q: Hashem is all-powerful. Does He really need our תפילות?

A: Hashem wants us to daven not for His sake, but for our sake!

Davening is our daily reminder that all our needs are provided for by Hashem. It is good for us to think about this. It trains us to turn to Hashem in times of need.

Write a story about a child who comes to realize that Hashem provides everything they need.

_____

_____

_____

_____

_____

_____

Q: The תפילה of מזמור לתודה is a song of thanks. It is meant to be said when one escapes a dangerous situation. So why do we say it every day?

A: Hashem does miracles for us every single day! He does so many miracles that we don't even pay attention to them. A miracle doesn't have to be an earth-shattering event; anything as predictable as the sun rising or as delicate as a butterfly's flapping wings is miraculous, if you think about it!

Write about something you find miraculous.

_____

_____

_____

_____

_____

What is your favorite תפילה and why?

Describe why it is meaningful to you.

קָרוֹב ה׳ לְכָל קֹרְאָיו לְכֹל אֲשֶׁר יִקְרָאֻהוּ בֶאֱמֶת

Hashem is close to all those who call out to Him; to all those who call out to Him in truth

The מעם לועז says that "אמת" stands for:

אַותיות: *letters*

מַילים: *words*

תַנועות: *emphasis*

If a person is careful about pronouncing the words correctly, then his תפילות will be answered.

Copy down one line from a תפילה in your סידור that you usually rush through. Pay attention to each letter and word as you write it down.

_____

_____

_____

When you daven this תפילה today, make sure you enunciate each letter properly.

We connect to Hashem through our actions.

Give examples of things we do to serve Him:

_____ _____

**But remember, actions alone are not enough.
We have to get our emotions involved.
Hashem wants us to *feel* excited about
serving Him!**

When we daven, our emotions "wake up" —
we connect to Hashem through our heart.

*How does davening lead us to feel close to
Hashem?*

_____

_____

מוח שליט על הלב

The mind rules over the heart

Learning leads to feeling.

When you daven, you train yourself to think about Hashem's greatness.
This helps you feel close to Him.

In which תפילות do we talk about Hashem's greatness?

_____

_____

_____

_____

_____

People are more likely to eat healthy food when it has a pleasing taste.

It is similar with davening — when your davening has a good 'taste', you will be more likely to commit yourself and enjoy your davening.

The 'taste' of davening is the meaning of the words. Understanding the words you are reciting transforms your davening experience. The תפילות will no longer be simply some words you *have* to say, but words you *want* to say!

Give yourself a "taste" of what you are saying every day! Can you translate the following words?

אדון: _____

עולם: _____

נשמה: _____

מלך: _____

יִשְׁתַּבַּח שִׁמְךְ לָעַד מַלְכֵּנוּ...
...בַּשָּׁמַיִם וּבָאָרֶץ....

"May your name be praised forever, our King...
in heaven and on earth."

*In the תפילה of ישתבח, we praise Hashem for
being King in heaven and on earth.
Over whom does He rule in each place?
What do you think is different about each
kingship?*

_____

_____

_____

_____

_____

_____

_____

A young boy once had a question for Rebbetzin Chana, the mother of the Lubavitcher Rebbe. "What is the Rebbe's favorite תפילה?" he asked. Rebbetzin Chana responded, "All the תפילות are important, but yes, there is one that must be more important than the rest. I will ask him and let you know."

The next week, she had an answer.

"It's a very short תפילה. It's the very first one we say in the morning! 'מודה אני לפניך'."

"That's it?" the boy asked.

"Yes, that's his favorite."

This תפילה became the boy's favorite as well. He later heard the Rebbe talking about מודה אני.

The Rebbe said that the message of this תפילה is that Hashem gives us another day of life every morning because He believes in us.

Why do we say מודה אני first thing in the morning?

The Baal Shem Tov used to say that he didn't know if he'd survive his davening each day, because he was so immersed in the service.

He got so overwhelmed with feelings of closeness to Hashem that he didn't know if his נשמה would stay in his body!

Have you ever felt closeness to Hashem? When did you experience it? What did it feel like?

_____

_____

_____

_____

_____

_____

_____

_____

חנן הנחבא was the son of the daughter of חוני המעגל. When the world was in need of rain, the sages would send the kindergarten children to him. They would grab his robe and beg: "Father, father, give us rain!"

Then he would turn to Hashem in prayer and say: "Master of the Universe! Send rain for the sake of these innocent children who do not know the difference between a Father who gives rain (that is, Hashem) and a father who does not give rain."

What is the lesson from this story and how can you apply it to your davening?

_____

_____

_____

_____

_____

_____

Imagine a teacher promises a reward to her students for a week of good behavior. What would she do if one or two students don't behave as they should?

The teacher may choose to overlook these incidents and still reward the entire class, since the majority deserve it.

This is why it is good to daven with a large group. Doing so awakens Hashem's compassion.

Even if some people deserve stricter judgment, Hashem will choose to bless *everyone* with kindness, simply because they are all together!

List three good things you have done today. When you daven, have in mind that they should be 'זכותים', merits, for others as well!

1. _____

2. _____

3. _____

Sometimes we hear about people suffering but we feel far removed from their pain.
This is one of the reasons we perform the מצוה of ביקור חולים, visiting the sick.
Seeing people in their pain reminds us to daven for them.

Write about a time you helped someone in pain.

_____

_____

_____

Today during davening, think about all the people who need a רפואה שלימה. You can write some names below.

_____

_____

_____

Many people turn to Hashem with lists of needs and desires.

Write a list of some of your most important wishes.

_____

_____

_____

_____

_____

_____

...But did you remember to include the most important wish on your list: Moshiach?

When Moshiach comes, you won't have to ask for anything else, because all your needs and desires will be taken care of!

If you knew that Moshiach was coming today, what would your davening look like?

It is best to ask Hashem to give us revealed good, and let Him decide how to help us, rather than 'advise' Him on what He should give us and when.

Write about a time you asked your parents for something. Did they decide to give it to you? Why or why not? Describe how it was ultimately for your best.

_____

_____

_____

_____

_____

_____

Draw a perfect circle.

On your own, it is nearly impossible to draw a perfect circle. Your lines may be wobbly. However, when you use a compass with the point firmly planted in the center, the circle is drawn easily.

When you keep Yiddishkeit as your center, you will have a happy, healthy and balanced life.

How does davening re-center you?

_____

_____

Davening is not a race.

If you were going for a meeting with the president, would you try to be out as fast as you can? Or would you try to make it last longer?

Sometimes people see others finishing davening quickly, and they try to hurry up so they don't feel behind. This is a mistake. Davening is not a race. It is a time to connect one-on-one with Hashem. Allow yourself to relax. You might even inspire others to slow down as well!

Did you ever slow down to enjoy an experience?

Today, take a few deep breaths before you begin davening. Picture yourself about to enter a peaceful room where you are alone with your Creator.

Q: Why can't our relationship with Hashem be automatic? Why do we have to put in work?

A: Hashem gives us a choice to have a relationship with him, because the best relationships are never forced. They require effort. Think about your closest friends. **You choose to spend time with each other.**

Hashem gives us the opportunity every day to "spend time" with Him. This is davening. When we daven, we're telling Hashem that we care about our relationship with Him and want to be close to Him.

What kind of effort do we need to put into our relationship with Hashem?

_____

_____

_____

_____

כי לא המטיר

(בראשית ב:ה)

Hashem had not caused it to rain

Why did Hashem not cause it to rain?

כי אדם אין לעבוד את האדמה

Because there was no man to work the ground.
Therefore, there was no one to recognize the benefit of rain.

Rashi teaches us that when אדם הראשון was created, he saw that it was necessary for the world to have rain. **So he davened for it and it fell, and then trees and plants grew.**

Why didn't Hashem make the rain fall right away?

Adapted excerpt of a letter from Rabbi Menachem Mendel Schneerson, the Lubavitcher Rebbe: 10th of Iyar 5725 (1965)

A Direct Pathway

"...Through davening and direct personal contact with Hashem, one is reminded every day that Hashem is not far away, in the Seventh Heaven, but is present and here, and His care extends to each and every person individually. This point has also been greatly emphasized by the Alter Rebbe in his book of Tanya, where he urges everyone to remember that 'והנה ה' נצב עליו' 'Behold, Hashem is standing near him.' With this in mind, there is no room left for any anxiety or worry, as דוד המלך said, 'ה' רועי לא אחסר' 'Hashem is my shepherd, I will not lack,' 'ה' לי לא אירא' 'Hashem is with me, I will not fear,' etc. Then, this is no longer a theoretical idea, but becomes a personal experience in the everyday life…"

Which words mean "and behold Hashem is standing over him"?

Rabbi Elazar said:

"מִיּוֹם שֶׁחָרַב בֵּית הַמִּקְדָּשׁ נִנְעֲלוּ שַׁעֲרֵי תְּפִלָּה"

Since the day the בית המקדש was destroyed, the gates of תפילה were locked and תפילות are not accepted as easily as they once were. But despite the fact that the gates of תפילה were locked,

"שַׁעֲרֵי דִמְעָה לֹא נִנְעֲלוּ",

the gates of tears have not been locked. One who cries before Hashem can rest assured that his תפילות will be answered, as it is stated:

"שִׁמְעָה תְפִלָּתִי ה'

וְשַׁוְעָתִי הַאֲזִינָה אֶל דִמְעָתִי אַל תֶּחֱרַשׁ"

"Hear my prayer, Hashem,
and listen to my pleading,
and don't be silent to my tears"

Why do you think Hashem answers תפילות said with tears?

_____

_____

_____

In the Gemara, Rabbi Chanin relates that Rabbi Chanina said:

"Anyone who prolongs his davening is assured that his תפילה will not return unanswered; it will surely be accepted."

From where do we see this? From משה רבינו.

He said: "וָאֶתְפַּלֵּל אֶל ה'" "And I davened to Hashem". Then, it is written "וַיִּשְׁמַע ה' אֵלַי" "And Hashem listened to me".

Write about a time Hashem answered your תפילה.

_____

_____

_____

_____

_____

Rabbi Chama, the son of Rabbi Chanina, said: A person who davened and saw that he was not answered, should daven again, as it is said:

"קַוֵּה אֶל ה' חֲזַק וְיַאֲמֵץ לִבֶּךָ וְקַוֵּה אֶל ה'"

"Hope in Hashem, strengthen yourself, let your heart take courage, and hope in Hashem"

Why does it say twice to "hope in Hashem"? So that we know we should turn to Hashem with hope, and if we need to we can turn to Him again.

Why do you think Hashem sometimes needs us to daven for a long time before we receive something?

_____

_____

_____

_____

_____

A piano requires regular tuning.

A car needs its tank to be filled with gas on a regular basis.

So too, the חכמים explain that there are four things which require constant strengthening:

1. תורה
2. מצוות
3. תפילה
4. דרך ארץ

Why do you think תפילה is one of the four areas that need constant strengthening?

_____

_____

_____

_____

Davening is like a ladder. It follows this process:

1. "הודאה": "Acknowledgment"

Recognizing, accepting, and appreciating Hashem's presence in this world, even if you don't fully understand it.

2. "שבח": "Praising"

Speaking about the details of Hashem's greatness and praising Him for all He does. This level brings you to a place of greater understanding.

3. "בקשה": "Asking"

On this rung of the ladder (when you are davening שמונה עשרה), you are standing like a servant before a master. At this high level of תפילה, your thoughts are completely devoted to Hashem. The purpose of davening for your personal needs is so that you have the tools to continue to serve Him.

Why is "בקשה" at the top of the ladder?

_____

_____

_____

הַכֹּל בִּידֵי שָׁמַיִם, חוּץ מִיִּרְאַת שָׁמַיִם

Everything is in the hands of Heaven,
except for יראת שמים (fear of Heaven)

Why do you think Hashem gave us the ability to choose to serve Him?

How does it make our עבודת ה' more valuable?

_____

_____

_____

_____

_____

_____

_____

_____

When you daven today, think about the fact that you are CHOOSING to connect to Hashem!

One day, a shepherd boy was passing by a Shul and heard people inside davening. He decided to join them.

However, he didn't know how to read. He saw them all davening with their סידורים. Not knowing what to do, he stood in the back of the Shul and yelled out "Aleph! Beis! Gimmel!" until he finished the entire Aleph Beis.

Some of the people davening got annoyed that he was disturbing their peace, so they went over to send him outside, when the Rabbi told them: **"Stop! That boy's shouting was more precious than any other תפילות said here today! His תפילה went straight to שמים!"**

~

Why do you think his תפילה went straight to שמים?

_____

_____

_____

When you experience difficulty concentrating during davening, slow down! Say each word with the patience and simplicity of a child just learning to read.

When distracting thoughts arise, gently try to push them aside. Pause for a moment and daven to Hashem to remove them.

Write a few sentences to ask Hashem to help you concentrate in your תפילה today.
Have this כוונה in mind while you daven.

_____

_____

_____

_____

_____

_____

Rabbi Yehoshua ben Levi said:
"Even an iron wall cannot separate the Jewish people from their Father in Heaven".
Draw a picture of תפילות soaring over an iron wall.

מִמַּעֲמַקִּים קְרָאתִיךָ ה׳

From the depths I called out to Hashem

One should not daven standing on a chair or in a high place, but rather in a low place, "from the depths".
Davening needs to come from a humble place.

Why do you think one needs to feel humble when davening before Hashem?

_____

_____

_____

_____

_____

_____

One of the חסידים of the Alter Rebbe was such a simple man that people didn't think he understood the meaning of the words he davened. Regardless, he davened for a very long time, even during the weekdays.

The חסידים were amazed that, even though he didn't understand much, he davened with passion and concentration. They finally decided to ask him about this. The man replied: "I only know that which I heard from the Alter Rebbe: זכור ושמור בדיבור אחד — The words "remember" and "guard" [the Shabbos] were stated by Hashem in one breath.' The Alter Rebbe explained this to mean: **One has to remember and guard in one's every word (breath) the אחד, the oneness of Hashem.**"

It was this thought from the Alter Rebbe Rebbe that energized his davening for forty years straight.

Why is it so powerful to think about Hashem's oneness?

Even if a sharp sword is resting on a person's neck, it should not stop them from davening to Hashem for mercy.

Give an example of a situation that could seem impossible to escape. Then think about how Hashem can intervene and save you.

_____

_____

_____

_____

_____

_____

_____

_____

_____

When you daven, remember:

‏"דע לפני מי אתה עומד"‎

"Know before Whom you are standing"

Create a 'flyer' on this topic with these words.

In the village of Premishlan, there was a steep hill leading up to the portion of the river that was used as the מקוה. People used to walk a longer route around the hill to avoid slipping. The only one who walked up the hill was Rabbi Meir of Premishlan. During the winter the ground was coated in ice, but he never slipped.

One day, two young men decided that they, too, would try to walk up the hill. They both fell and injured themselves badly. That was when they realized that Rabbi Meir must be a special man.
"How come you never slip?" they asked him.

"When a man is connected above," said Rabbi Meir, "he doesn't stumble below."

What lesson do you think Rabbi Meir was trying to teach them? (Connect to davening.)

_____

_____

_____

_____

Can you imagine the pride you would feel if you found that a famous person visiting your city wants to stay in your house?

You would likely immediately begin preparations to make his stay as comfortable as possible.

Guess what? This happens every day! Hashem could have created any dwelling place for Himself, but he wants *you* to 'host' him!

~~~

Write 4 things you will do to make a דירה בתחתונים, a 'home' for Hashem, today.

1. _____

2. _____

3. _____

4. _____

When you daven today, think about the great privilege and honor you have to be a 'host' for Hashem.

דַּע מַה לְמַעְלָה מִמְּךָ, עַיִן רוֹאָה וְאֹזֶן שׁוֹמַעַת וְכָל מַעֲשֶׂיךָ בַּסֵּפֶר נִכְתָּבִין

"Know all that there is above you: an eye that sees, an ear that hears, and that all your actions are written in a book."

Do you find it easy or difficult to remember that Hashem is always watching you?
Write about what you can do to keep this in mind while you daven.

_____

_____

_____

_____

_____

_____

_____

_____

וַיַּשְׁכֵּם אַבְרָהָם בַּבֹּקֶר אֶל הַמָּקוֹם אֲשֶׁר עָמַד שָׁם

"And Avraham got up in the morning to the place where he stood"

(בראשית יט:כז)

Avraham was the first person to daven שחרית.

Why do you think it is important to daven specifically in the morning?

_____

_____

_____

_____

_____

_____

_____

וַיֵּצֵא יִצְחָק לָשׂוּחַ בַּשָּׂדֶה לִפְנוֹת עָרֶב

"And Yitzchak went out to converse in the field towards evening"

(בראשית כד:סג)

Yitzchak was the first person to daven מנחה. He went into the field to daven as he waited to meet Rivka, his future wife.

Why do you think it is precious to Hashem when we daven to Him in the afternoon?

_____

_____

_____

_____

_____

_____

וַיִּפְגַּע בַּמָּקוֹם וַיָּלֶן שָׁם

"And he [Yaakov] encountered the place, and he slept there"
(בראשית כח:יא)

Yaakov was the first person to daven מעריב, in the place where he lay down to sleep with stones around his head.

Why do you think it is important to daven in the evening?

_____

`

_____

_____

_____

_____

_____

A little girl went on a walk with her friends and got lost in the forest. No one knew where she had disappeared to. The town sent out a search team to look for her. Her father, desperate to find his daughter, led the search team, but no one could find her anywhere. The sun set, and the search team decided to pause and continue in the morning daylight.

The girl was terrified to be alone in the forest at night. Sitting on a log, she began to cry. She wept and wailed, hoping that someone would hear her and rescue her.

Little did she know that her father was indeed in the forest. He was the only one who decided to stay and search through the nighttime. Suddenly, the girl heard a sound. She woke up, startled. **When she saw the face of her father, she cried out, "Abba! I found you!"**

Connect this story to davening.

A businessman heard the Maggid of Mezeritch would spend hours davening. He wondered why it took him so long. After all, he had the same כוונות in mind when he davened. So he decided to take a detour on his annual trip to Leipzig to find out. "Why does it take you so long to daven?" he asked the Maggid of Mezeritch. "I have the same כוונות in mind when I daven, but it doesn't take me nearly as much time as it does you."

The Maggid responded with another question. "How do you make a living?"

"I go to Leipzig to buy merchandise, and then bring it back to my town and sell it there."

"How do you know you made a profit?"

"I keep a special notebook with all the expenses and income recorded."

"So why go to the market? Just fill out your notebook and you'll earn money that way!" the Maggid responded. The man burst out laughing. "You don't earn money by writing down numbers! You need to actually go!"

"Davening is the same," said the Maggid. "Just going through the motions and reciting the words is not enough. **You need to actually 'make the journey', investing your heart and mind into it."**

Underline the businessman's question. ¹⁷³

Inspiration is like a spark.

It doesn't last long unless you *do* something with it. You have to translate it into action!

To do this, you must be constantly aware of where you are holding in your 'עבודת ה, and know what you seek to accomplish.

Write a few sentences about an area of Yiddishkeit you would like to improve in today.

_____

_____

_____

_____

In which section of davening will you focus on the above?

_____

A villager became ill.

The doctor wrote a prescription to be given three times a day, dissolved in water.

The man's wife tore the prescription into tiny pieces, dissolved it one piece at a time, and gave the concoction to the man to drink.

When the patient grew sicker, they rushed him to the doctor. He asked for the medication.

They said, "The prescription is used up."

When they explained what they had done, the doctor was stunned.

"Can a person be healed by placing paper in his mouth? If he would have had the medicine he would have been cured."

Connect this story to davening.

Rabbi Shimon said:

"Be careful with קריאת שמע and תפילה. And when you daven, do not make your davening something routine, but a plea for compassion before Hashem."

Why?

"כִּי חַנּוּן וְרַחוּם הוּא אֶרֶךְ אַפַּיִם וְרַב חֶסֶד וְנִחָם עַל הָרָעָה"

"For He [Hashem] is gracious and compassionate, slow to anger, generous in kindness, and renouncing punishment"

Describe what it means to "plea for compassion" before Hashem.

_____

_____

_____

_____

Rabbi Yitzchak said:

"For what reason did our אבות originally not have children?

"Hashem wanted them to daven for children, since He desires the תפילות of צדיקים."

Why do you think Hashem wants to hear our תפילות?

_____

_____

_____

_____

_____

_____

_____

וּקְרָאתֶם אֹתִי וַהֲלַכְתֶּם וְהִתְפַּלַּלְתֶּם אֵלָי וְשָׁמַעְתִּי אֲלֵיכֶם:

ירמיהו כט:יב

"When you call me and go and daven to me, I will listen to you"

Hashem promises that He will answer you when you reach out to him.

רש"י explains that the word "והלכתם" refers to "and you go"... in My ways. Meaning, when we follow in Hashem's ways, we are **guaranteed** that He will answer us when we call out to Him!

So, davening accomplishes a twofold effect:

1) Gives us a chance to ask for our needs

2) Gives us a chance to connect to Hashem and strengthen our commitment to תורה ומצוות — which will open the channels for us to receive the ברכות we ask for!

Where in davening do we ask Hashem to help us follow in His ways?

וּבִקַּשְׁתֶּם אֹתִי וּמְצָאתֶם כִּי תִדְרְשֻׁנִי בְּכָל־לְבַבְכֶם

ירמיהו כט:יג

"And you will search for me, and you will find me; if you search with your whole heart."

When you daven today, envision yourself searching for Hashem.

Where can you search for Hashem?
And why does He hide Himself — for His sake or ours? Explain.

_____

_____

_____

_____

_____

_____

The Tzemach Tzedek told his חסידים:

"The Baal Shem Tov loved light, so his students always made sure to light many candles around him. Once, they only had one candle and couldn't get any more. They felt disappointed that they couldn't provide him with the light he loved.

"When the Baal Shem Tov walked in, he told his students to go outside and gather icicles. The ice burned like wax, and the room was bathed in light."

The Tzemach Tzedek was quiet. Then, he said: "For the Baal Shem Tov's חסידים, ice burned and brought forth light. Today's חסידים sit in warm, well-lit rooms, and it is still dark and cold..."

What do you think is the difference between a "warm" davening and a "cold" davening?

_____

_____

רֵאשִׁית הַיְרִידָה, רַחֲמָנָא לִצְלַן, הוּא הֶעְדֵּר
הָעֲבוֹדָה בִּתְפִלָּה

The first stage in a person's spiritual decline, חס
ושלום, is a lack of effort when serving Hashem
with davening. Everything becomes dry and
cold… Even the routine performance of מצוות
becomes a burden. One does מצוות in a hurry
and loses excitement for learning תורה. The
very atmosphere becomes more about the
physical. And it is understood that a person in
such a state cannot be a positive influence on
others at all.

*Why do you think a loss of excitement in
davening is the first sign that a person is חס
ושלום losing interest in תורה and מצוות?*

_____

_____

_____

_____

Congratulations on completing 180 days of davening journaling!

Has davening become more meaningful to you this year? Describe how you feel your perspective on davening has changed, or how something new you learned has made an impact on you.

_____

_____

_____

_____

_____

_____

_____

_____

_____